The Pulchritude Of Secrets

By Grace D. Pickard

1

Attached

Warm is the day

When my thoughts are at bay

When I'm breathing you in

Like you're my sin

Warm is the day

When I don't know what to say

When I'm watching you grin

Like you're my sin

Warm is the day

When the sky is all gray

When I'm missing your skin

Like you're my sin

Warm is the day

When you're far away

When you wonder where I've been

Like I'm your only sin

A Haiku For You

Green with hazel specks

Your eyes envision profound

Not reconnaissance

La lune

Looking over your shoulder at the moon

I decry our thousands of dazzling years

Don't let me go- this life is anew.

We could change the endings tears-

Perchance this life is opportune.

Or maybe we're involuntary volunteers

We are pulling apart....

Say goodbye to my heart.

Time

Huge green eyes stared back at me,

We talked and chatted-

Due to the immediate attraction.

Gaining courage I wrote him a note;

"Will you be mine?"

Discouraging, out came from his throat;

"I already have a valentine"

I accepted it was not our time

That summer I kept him a friend

We grew very close

And towards summers end

He wanted me

one could suppose

But I was no longer interested

He accepted it was not our time

We didn't talk for a month or two

Though unlike me- he was persistent

Then one day I gave into "You"

He stole my first kiss- I was nonresistant

Finally the time seemed right

I let my vulnerable heart ignite

A month was fantastic

I was so naïve

Quite a while had pass'd

Until I realized I had just been deceived;

"I thought it was just a friend fling"

It wasn't our time and I *wasn't* accepting

I cut off all communication- protecting

Years flew by

But one September day

He decided to say "Hi"

We rekindled and put old thoughts at bay

Best best friends we became

Yet old attraction didn't die

Are we finally both on the same page-

Is the world saying it's time?

Or is this just another lessons stage?

If it is the latter,

I do not believe my heart can accept it.

Perchance I'm Ready

The one who destroyed

Is the only one I want to be with

Open my heart to him

Let my broken trust escort him

I think I'm ready to commit

A Haiku For You

Stomach butterflies

Blushing rose, red in disguise

Flutter when you're near

Romeo

A man, with a depression struck face;

who spent his days hidden away

now tries to erase

his hearts clouds of gray

His friends did him a favor

in effort to mend his soul

Yet his heart was the craver-

Juliet made him whole

He spoke as though he was creeper

she was swooned by his smile

Married off and he tried to keep her

killed her cousin; subjected to exile

While away, Juliet had a plan to fake her death

Little did she know she was taking Romeo's last breath

My ticking clock

My heart

Is so tender

'Tis fragile- made of glass

'Tis longing appreciation

Amour

Beirut

You were awkward

Oh so adorable

Linky and upward

Not close to normal

I had grown; reached your height

You had muscles

And you kissed me goodnight

Filling me with bubbles

Now you're taller,

Still incredibly cute.

Yet, quite the player;

I'd be invisible to you even in Beirut

Ambiguously Undefined

We're just like Carrie and Mr. Big

You want to be free

We're just like Harry and Sally

We like each other at the wrong times

We're just like Lloyd and Diane

I'll never stop trying

We're just like Allie and Noah

From different walks of life

We're just like Scarlett and Rhett

Independent and Fickle

We're just like Ilsa and Rick

Nothing can separate us forever

We're just like Bridget and Mark

Childhood friends turned accidental lovers

We're just like Hubbell and Katie

I'm just too mysterious to settle
down with

We're just like you and me

Undefined and unique

A Haiku For You

You, Sir, are clarity

Yet your mind wanders aloof;

Sun, clear opacity.

Aging

It disturbs me that we talk to each other like strangers

That because I'm a girl you treat me differently

That the income of our future is

important

That how many girls digits you got shows

your popularity

That love is not based on connection- but superficiality

Since when did we grow up?

Who stole our innocence?

Let's leave behind everyone else

And enjoy ourselves

I am the sun

I am the sun

I might burn you

But only with puns

I am the sun

I'll enlighten you

Yet I won't be done

I am the sun

I will brighten your path

Just for fun

I am the sun

I will keep the moon bright

Because you are the one

I am the sun

If you come too close to me

I will burn you, loved one

Confusing Clarity

I confuse you- I'm so strange

You clear my mind- you're unbiased

You confuse me- you change often

I clear your mind- I show you the deeper side

The Nitty-Gritty

Here's the truth

It kills me seeing you with all these girls

Knowing it isn't me

Here's the truth

I should've spent all of my time with you

When you were available

Here's the truth

I've always loved you

And that will last through all of my lives

Here's the truth:

I really just miss you.

Dandy

Vulnerability

The certitude that all will be swell

Will I be fine and dandy?

Heartwood

I am a tree

Sprouting leaves

But my leaves too will leave

I am a tree

My thick bark protects me

But contains deep scars

Beneath my bark are layers of life

The history of my surroundings

But my heartwood is dead

My heartwood still supports me

It won't decay or lose strength

But it's only because of my thick bark

My outer bark- gained over decades;

Protects me from the destruction of my

Heartwood

For being

Vulnerable

Un Haïku Pour Vous

La fille est très belle

Il veut la fille avec les yeux (bleus)

Elle ne réalise pas

Who's to blame

I can't keep grounded

My soul is aloof

And It's because of you

I want to let go

But I'm keeping myself here

And it's because of you

I see you

And I'm green with envy

And it's because of me

I remember

I wrecked all possibilities

And it's because of me

Untitled

The smell of daisies

The soul drifts through a valley

The sun warms the heart

F.14

In February the sun shines bright,

Sending me letters

About her burnt orange light

In February the grass turns green,

Envious of my toes

Cuddling the blades in between

In February the light, purple flowers

Freshly planted

Are optimistic for rain showers

In February my heart and mind

Don't race and worry

Because life is perfectly aligned

A Haiku For Me

Optimistic girl

Radiate positive thoughts

Break through the abyss

Prima

My prime example of love:

Stemmed from intensity,

Is not a one size fits all glove.

They found each other- destiny:

In the midst of a celebration,

In high school unintentionally.

Born with high expectations, I think:

Maybe my soulmate is nearing,

I'm just waiting for my invitation.

The truth is- it's unsparing;

Waiting around for 'the one',

Takes away my caring.

Ditto

One word

You said "ditto"

That word shattered my heart

Because it took courage to say

(I) love you

A Haiku For You

Listen to my sorrow-

Understand my oppressed mind-

Comprehend regret.

Anger is my mask

I look at her picture

I am disgusted

I make fun of her figure

Not robusted

She looks like a child

Such an innocent smile

While I'm just wild

And not worthwhile

She's flexible

A ballerina

I'm sensual

Not from Galena

The hatred towards her

Is the jealousy in me

I'm full of sorrow

Because I'm incomplete

And being angry is easier than showing

I am weak

Un poeme pour vous

La vie c'elle noire

Mais ma vie est belle

Noire et belle et triste

Misconstrued

Villainy ambiguous

Inside or outside, you or me

It's all misconstrued

A Haiku For me

Freedom is within me,

The heart confined belongs to me.

The key- Perception.

Mass produced

Long ago I dreamt

I imagined we lived happily

While together we slept

Our minds were full of capacity

Intertwined and squeezed tight

Only tragedy could exhaust reality

Woe announced herself alive

Teaching him to look elsewhere

For I wasn't in a false disguise

I tried to change and reappear

Though, he prefers girls of cookie cutter

The game became crystal clear

Men choose the fallen apples,

Why climb for something of substantial?

Repugnant

You see me and scowl

I'm weird and crazy

And sometimes I even howl

I'm abnormal- quite the mazy

But, I'm not hot enough for your prowl

I'm awkwardly shaped; though not lazy

You find me repugnant and foul-

That's how you've made me feel lately

But I don't bite! I don't even growl!

Ah Just call me Gracie

Don't

Don't look at me you fool

Recklessly you lead astray my heart

Uttering softly goodbye

Desiccant Glue

Numb is the girl who dreams

        The one who fails to see everything

Even though the world is not all that it seems

        She finds the beauty in anything

Dumb is the boy who leaves

        The one who is burying

A life he is told not to believe

        Who will just continue worrying

Numb is the girl who loves

        Who cries tears of gold-

Over just one silly dove-

        Who thought she was too bold

Dumb is the boy who is beloved

        Who had been told

"A proper man is devoid of-

      Girls who aren't bought and sold'

Dumb is the boy who never knew

            She was his only glue

Choices

Here's the thing about second chances;

After the first, you're just being used

No matter what he says and dances

Your sweet personality is abused

When one can't let go

Waiting for the right moment

Feeling oh so low

Becoming more than broken

He manipulates

But karma never reciprocates

Crying- being vulnerable

He apprehends

While you're not able

To comprehend

Seeking a lover

Or perhaps just being lonely

He starts to smother

But it's him being phony

He manipulates

But karma never reciprocates

Polar Opposites

Manipulation

Blind beastly

Destroying, aching, rebirthing

Leading, taking, generous, mutual

Giving, following, reflecting

Love

A Haiku for You

One night's all it took

I am still in love with you

Greater is the wound

A Haiku For Me

I am captured

Inside the cage I am his prey

The gate is wide open

Yellow Billed

I know I must leave

This is intoxication

Do not squeeze me tight

Like a magpie let me fly

Drifting effervescently

One text

What am I doing?

Waiting here for you to care?

Beep..beep.. My heart stops-

Read, type, send, wait for a reply.

Stuck on you- stringing along.

Lemon

Biting-Yellow-Juicy-

Vibrant, cold, pain inducing,

Life is a lemon

Liberation from Attachments

Cold is the day

When I know I can't stay

When I'm waving goodbye

Knowing it can't be I

Cold is the day

When the world is made of clay

When I know I can't cry

Because it was all a lie

Cold is the day

When you're crawling back in May

When it's only just *i*

And I can't live any more lies

2

Freedom

Tonight I have decided

That love should be indicted

Because I am not the final "Z"

But alas I am free.

Yesterday I said goodbye

I'm deserving of a wise guy

Because I am not a bourgeois

But alas I am free.

Tomorrow I may just weep

It's hard to feel incomplete

Yes, I don't flow like ocean sea

But alas I am free

Currently I am exultant

For this is the resultant

I am a bel esprit

(But) Alas I am free

élan vital

My soul

Is happy now

Uncaged, allowed to roam

It sees life's utter pulchritude

I'm free

Violin

Music is life

But love will suffice

                                      Except violin is my passion

                                      So both are of satisfaction

Rebirthed from love

Discovering myself again is quite exciting;

Ripping apart the past-

Understanding myself through writing-

Kicking out the unsurpassed-

Hellish thoughts not biting

And making an impact.

Love was not lost

Love was created by me, heartbroken and distraught

Me versus me

Last year

Clingy desperate

Annoying, longing, controlling

Behind, manipulated, positive, joyful

Leading, attracting, realizing

Today

A Haiku Truly For You

You up there! Hello!

This is a haiku for you-

You are beautiful!

No

This is not right

                                                            It's quite left

I need you

                                                            To apologize

To keep me and hold me tight

                                        You'll feel the sudden fright

                        No

Final 12w

Sometimes you have to let go-

When time moves quicker than you.

Sartre Says

Breathe in this moment

Leave behind; don't look ahead

Be here presently

Drifting to dream

I put on Harvest Moon

Neil Young wraps me in his arms

The music makes me swoon

Dulls out the loud alarms

Breathe in

I am in a valley beneath one tree

The earth hugs me with grass

Wind calls to address me

"This all shall pass"

Breathe out

My tears pitter patter like rain drops

Soaking my memories with confusion

Every fact hurls through mid air and stops

This rainstorm had no preclusion

Breathe in

Imagining us far apart in separate whens

Both living- saying adieu

"I want to see you dance again

Because I am still in love with you"

Breathe out

No matter the shatter, I must keep trying

Give me the power to overcome

I can stop myself from internally dying

And bring back what isn't numb

Breathe in

Listen to my somber melody

Connect with my bitter bones

Appreciate my new identity

Walk with me into the unknown

I am alive

I am alive

Here is my unadulterated heart

Smash it, squeeze it, make the blood ooze out

The scary bits of possible rejection

This is vulnerability.

Bits and pieces

I have parted ways with my body

Because my mind isn't present

My heart, a charcoal gray: foggy

Has little passion since our dissent

I wrote dainty letters for you

Romantic, lengthy confessions.

Every empty word- away each flew

Whilst wading daily in depression.

Softly my soul fades with my love.

A hollow hole cut deep in your heart-

By unkind hope: an olive branching dove--

Is the coal that fuels this hatred art.

This suffering manifests my mind.

Winds blustering my common sense,

And life muttering "Are you blind?"

My body is combusting in defense .

Revenge begs me to set you ablaze-

Compassion treads across this hell,

Speaks and heads into the insane,

Pulls me by the threads out of a spell.

I want you to be happy!

I restrain from you- I am free -

I won't mention your infidelity.

Just make me feel not absentee.

I'm done being unhappy.

A Part Of Me Will Die

At some point the mind must release

And allow the pain to subside

To make tomorrow settle for peace

With the salty waves in my mind

At some point the mind must let go

And forget about the weeks and days

Spent upon the ocean's ebb and flow

Let go he rains the hearts fiery blaze

At some point the heart must warm up

And angered she burns quickly

Boiling the polluted puddles into sirup

Which leaks into the soul thickly

At some point part of the soul must die

Allowing the whole to be free

She will be vulnerable and cry

But alas she can genuinely be

Couplet shins

All of these old emotions,

Solidify my heart's devotions.

Haunts

Your presence haunts me-

Unconsciously, in my mind:

Altering my reality-

Nonexistent in yours.

Untitled Haiku

Here's what I hold true:

My feelings for you remain.

perspicacity

Mayday, Mayday

In May the flowers have wilted;

The sky is heavy, looming-

Waiting to be tilted-

Waiting for the clouds to be consuming-

The tears that winter left-

Of those who could not stay warm.

Their hearts; stolen by theft:

Because they too could not conform.

In May the birds are silent,

Theirs songs have gone unheard.

Everyone has been compliant,

In a world quite absurd.

In May the morning air is polluted-

Stuck in thick clouds, particles unmoving.

The whole concept is convoluted-

Makes me feel dark and brooding.

In May the sun is gelid;

Her golden swords pulverize,

(Whilst they descent, Earth gives forbid.)

Like delicate, sapphire butterflies,

Whose wings flutter until exhaust-

Hurling down singing sweet lullabies,

Carelessly into springs frost.

Cervidae

Doe eyed and vial she is stopped,

He lifts up his weapon and directs it-

The bullet blows-glides toward the shocked:

In that moment his heart is lit.

She stares back at him frightened,

Knowing he is her last moment.

By their connection he is enlightened,

Knowing he is her last opponent.

He falls on his knees-

Realizing the consequence.

Begging time with pleas-

To give him a conscience.

She breathes out her worries-

And assumes her final end:

Exhaling love for the forest and it's flurries-

She excuses him from being condemned.

They lock eyes in sorrow,

While the shattered air kills their innocence.

Because there isn't a tomorrow-

In her world of his insolence.

May 15

Dialing your number is forbidden

Blocked, deleted, out-of-mind, hidden

Tomorrow is unwritten

But I sense a gloom a thicken

The sorrow will never leave this valley of smitten

Raw emotions scare you, chicken

Not City Stars

You are the city

I am trying to get back into nature.

Your bright lights beckon me back-

But, you're the pollution that is killing me.

City officials refuse to address the problem-

Even when I write up a petition and policy-

to highlight the issues-

I am ignored.

There are natural bright lights in nature

- the ones I miss-

life with fresh air is positivity.

It's my fault I allowed the city to become

polluted.

Coracinus

Once the world was inhabited by ravens,

Who perched on the trees limbs-

Shading all of earth's nations.

They committed many sins:

Withholding all forms of endearment.

Yet pecked earth and gave her grins.

Solidifying became a determinant.

She swelled up- holding in her sorrows.

Her garden became incoherent.

The ravens flew to the zenith of Kilimanjaro,

Stopped in awe and courted the sun-

Everything became romanced with tomorrow.

Earth rained down like a machine gun-

When the ravens gloated.

But, she decided she wasn't done.

Months went by while she was devoted,

Depressed and dying,

The ravens didn't even notice.

Her landscapes went black during her lying.

Shiny, black, charcoal essence;

Became of herself although, she was trying.

She decided to let go of her adolescence,

Send the ravens away-

Creating their fast evanescence.

Forever the raven lingered in her garden,

Because her love for them is not forgotten.

Contiguous

I am the water that trickles down your throat:

With each gulp you drink into me- I satiate.

I am the air your lungs breathe in and out:

Filling each breath only to be expelled consistently.

I am the empty space between your blinks:

The lacuna that widens your range of sight.

I am the sun that beats down on your coat:

Nourishing your cold bones- becoming emaciated.

I am the moon pulling the ocean in and out:

Mystifying your unmitigated thought persistently.

I am the matter surrounding all you think-

Which must cause you quite the horrid fright.

Love breathes into life;

Without life, love dies.

Love

a tree sprouts new leaves every year,

supporting each delicate, envious sprout

she is patient

they discuss life without conscious,

and emotions without expression.

They use the light to enrich their lives,

until the darkness sweeps over them in the heat of winter.

Orange, brown- crumbling with the wind

The tree must let go of what was herself...

waiting for her next blossoming.

Goodbye, Officially. Hello, Grace.

It is not the stale summer air that settles my emotions,

Rather it is the soft glance towards freedom

As I, too, am a wanderer within myself-

Foggy eyed I stare at a now nameless figure

Blue eyed, brown hair, wasting away in self-created starvation

starvation from love

starvation from happiness

starvation from passion

starvation from a so called reality

Toes are miles away from my conscious

Shins are recognized in the mirror

Knees are relaxed connected to the thighs

belly button perfectly inline with the freckle between my breasts

collarbone, neck, chin, mouth, eyes-

EYES staring into me, into me, to me,me

I

Turn away- don't recognize

eyes-I

eyes to drown within oneself

to live within white clarity and bitter blue

to be expelled onto scarlet cheeks

and evaporate into nothingness

Tears are me swimming through waves of you

I-

I am to resist evaporation

I am free to be me

I am to release my sorrows

and I am not sorry

I am not apologizing

I am not seeping into the cold, darkness of nothingness-

That is loving you

Coup de grâce

I saw her

My lip quivered

And my heart stopped

I saw her

The earth fell

And crashed into the abyss

I saw her

Realizing the chaos

As it shattered from her glimpse

I saw her

Looking into me

And regarding my essence

I saw her

Eyes piercing me

And I was petrified by her kindness

I saw her

Breathed in death

And the last of all beautiful things was seen

www.ingramcontent.com/pod-product-compliance
Lightning Source LLC
Chambersburg PA
CBHW031456040426
42444CB00007B/1127